The Sporting Life

by Will Bullas

chimp shot...

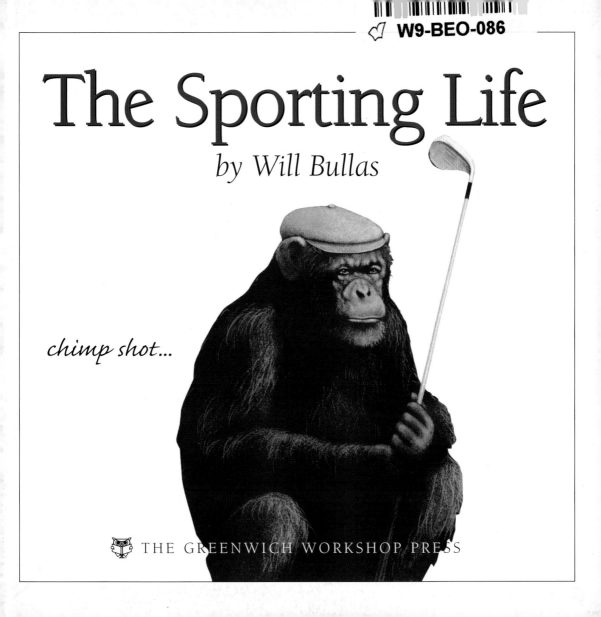

THE GREENWICH WORKSHOP PRESS

A GREENWICH WORKSHOP PRESS BOOK

Copyright ©2001 by The Greenwich Workshop Press
All art ©Will Bullas

Published by the Greenwich Workshop Press. One Greenwich Place, P.O. Box 875, Shelton, CT 06484. (203) 925-0131 or (800) 243-4246.

Library of Congress Cataloging-in-Publication Data
Bullas, Will, 1949-
      The sporting life / by Will Bullas
          p. cm.
ISBN 0-86713-069-5 (alk. paper)
      1. Bullas, Will, 1949- 2. Sports in art. 3. Animals in art. 4. American wit and humor,
Pictorial. I. Title

ND1839.B77 A4 2001
759.13--dc21

2001040305

Limited edition prints and canvas reproductions, and figurines based on Will Bullas' paintings, are available exclusively through The Greenwich Workshop, Inc. and its 1200 dealers in North America. Collectors interested in obtaining information on available releases and the location of their nearest dealer are requested to visit our website at **www.greenwichworkshop.com** or to write or call the publisher at the address above.

Jacket front: (l to r) the home team..., ski bunny..., aquaduck..., chimp shot..., fowl ball..., pigskin...
Book design by Sheryl P. Kober
Printed in Singapore by Imago
First Printing 2001
2   3 4 5   04 03 02 01

Play with the fools of the game...

The sporting life is not just about doing well and winning, it's about who's in the game. For humorist Will Bullas the players are a runner duck, frog, pig, elephant and few other chumps who stand in for us humans. There are plenty of highjinks as Bullas turns the tables on some of our favorite pastimes from *first and ten...* to *the yoga of fly-fishing....* Who can compete with a web-footed swim team? It's all in good sport, with nonsense and fun, as we play with the serious business of sports. Are you game?

aqua duck...

high diver...

peanut putter...

fore...ever

no where to hide...

the backquackers...

the swim team...

the feather weight...

the gallery...

first and ten...

soccer Mom...

mixed doubles...

the home team...

open season...

hareball...

a day at the races...

tennis anyone?

puck duck...

pigskin...

fowl ball...

hareline fracture...

wet and wild...

surf quacks...

the snow bunny...

water hazard...

putts...

*the yoga
of flyfishing...*

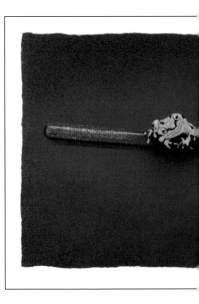

putter peeper...

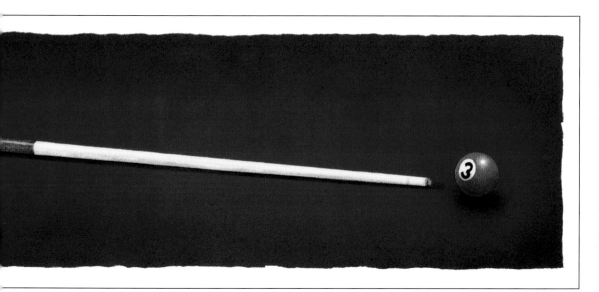

the pool man...

a little snorkeling...

helmet hare...

fishing
stories...
the tuna...

hoo's on first?

urban

bungee...